THE ELISE ECKLUND SONGBOOK

ISBN: 978-1-5400-6763-0

HAL•LEONARD®

Visit Hal Leonard Online at
www.halleonard.com

Contact us:
Hal Leonard
7777 West Bluemound Road
Milwaukee, WI 53213
Email: info@halleonard.com

In Europe, contact:
Hal Leonard Europe Limited
42 Wigmore Street
Marylebone, London, W1U 2RY
Email: info@halleonardeurope.com

In Australia, contact:
Hal Leonard Australia Pty. Ltd.
4 Lentara Court
Cheltenham, Victoria, 3192 Australia
Email: info@halleonard.com.au

PREFACE 5

STRUMMING PATTERN KEY 6

BELLYACHE Billie Eilish 7

CAN'T HELP FALLING IN LOVE Twenty One Pilots 10

DEMONS Imagine Dragons 12

HEY, SOUL SISTER Train 16

I'M YOURS Jason Mraz 24

ME! Taylor Swift ft. Brendon Urie 20

OCEAN EYES Billie Eilish 27

OVER THE RAINBOW IZ 30

PHOTOGRAPH Ed Sheeran 33

SHAPE OF YOU Ed Sheeran 36

Music is a huge part of my life. It has brought me so much joy, connected me with amazing people, and given me crazy opportunities. Ukulele is an instrument that I had always been interested in learning, and I finally took the plunge at 19 years old to pick it up. I instantly fell in love with the bright, happy sound and started learning all of my favorite songs on it. I love that a lot of the chords are simple to play with some practice, so pretty much anyone can enjoy learning it.

I wanted to compile a book of some of my favorite songs to play on uke with chords and strumming patterns so you can have a resource to get started or further your journey. These songs are absolute bops and so, so fun to play and sing along to! Set aside time to practise, take it slow, and have a good time! Happy strumming! ☺

Elise Ecklund

STRUMMING PATTERNS KEY

D - down strum
U - up strum
X - mute

BELLYACHE

WORDS AND MUSIC BY BILLIE EILISH AND FINNEAS O'CONNELL

STRUMMING PATTERNS
Single down strums
D UUD UUD DU
D UXX UXU DDU

C   Am   Em

Intro | C | Am | Em | |

Verse 1

C
Sittin' all alone,

Am
Mouth full of gum

Em
In the driveway.

C
My friends aren't far

Am
In the back of my car

Em
Lay their bodies.

Pre-Chorus 1

          C   Am
Where's my mi - nd?

         Em
Where's my mi - nd?

Verse 2

                  C
They'll be here pretty soon,

  Am   **Em**
Lookin' through my room for the money.

        C
I'm bitin' my nails,

      Am
I'm too young to go to jail.

        Em
It's kinda funny.

Pre-Chorus 2

          C   **Am**
Where's my mi - nd?

       Em
Where's my mi - nd?

          C   **Am**
Where's my mi - nd?

       Em
Where's my mi - nd?

Chorus

                  C   **Am**
Maybe it's in the gutter where I left my lover,

             Em
What an expensive fate.

          C
My V is for Vendetta,

             Am
Thought that I'd feel better.

                    Em
But now I got a bellyache.

Verse 3

    C   **Am**
Everything I do, the way I wear my noose

        Em
Like a necklace.

    C   **Am**
I wanna make 'em scared like I could be anywhere

             Em
Like I'm wreck-less.

Pre-Chorus 3

         C   Am
I lost my mi - nd.

         Em
I don't mi - nd.

         C   Am
Where's my mi - nd?

         Em
Where's my mind?

Chorus

         C   Am
Maybe it's in the gutter where I left my lover,

         Em
What an expensive fate.

         C
My V is for Vendetta,

         Am
Thought that I'd feel better.

         Em
But now I got a bellyache.

         C   Am
Maybe it's in the gutter where I left my lover,

         Em
What an expensive fate.

         C
My V is for Vendetta,

         Am
Thought that I'd feel better.

         Em
But now I got a bellyache.

CAN'T HELP FALLING IN LOVE

WORDS AND MUSIC BY GEORGE DAVID WEISS, HUGO PERETTI AND LUIGI CREATORE

> **STRUMMING PATTERNS**
> Single down strums
> D DUDU

C Em Am F G B7 A7 Dm

Intro　　| C　　　　　|　　　　　|

Verse 1
　　　　C　　Em　Am
　　　　Wise　men　say,

　　　　　　　　F　　C　G
　　　　'Only fools　rush　in'

　　　　　　F　G　　Am　F　　　C　G　C
　　　　But I　can't　help　falling in love　with　you.

Verse 2
　　　　C　　Em Am
　　　　Shall　I　stay,

　　　　　　　　F　C　G
　　　　Would it be　a　sin?

　　　　　　F　G　　Am　F　　　C　G　C
　　　　If I　can't　help　falling in love　with　you.

Bridge
　　　　Em　　　　　　B7
　　　　　Like the river flows,

　　　　Em　　　　　　B7
　　　　　Shortly to the sea.

　　　　Em　　　　　　B7
　　　　　Darling, so we go

　　　　　　　A7　　　　　　Dm　G
　　　　Some things were meant to be.

Verse 3

```
        C     Em   Am
        Take  my   hand,

                   F     C    G
        Take my whole  life   too.

                F    G    Am   F       C    G    C
        'Cause I  can't help falling in love  with you.
```

Bridge

```
        Em                   B7
          Like the river flows,

        Em                   B7
          Shortly to the sea.

        Em                   B7
          Darling, so we go

                A7                       Dm   G
        Some things were meant to be.
```

Verse 4

```
        C     Em   Am
        Take  my   hand,

                   F     C    G
        Take my whole  life   too.

                F    G    Am   F       C    G    C
        'Cause I  can't help falling in love  with you.

                F    G    Am   F       C    G    C
        'Cause I  can't help falling in love  with you.
```

DEMONS

WORDS AND MUSIC BY DANIEL REYNOLDS, BENJAMIN MCKEE,
DANIEL SERMON, ALEXANDER GRANT AND JOSH MOSSER

STRUMMING PATTERNS
Single down strums
DDDU
DDD UUD DDU

To match original recording, place capo on 3rd fret

Verse 1

C
When the days are cold

G
And the cards all fold

Am
And the saints we see

F
Are all made of gold

C
When your dreams all fail

G
And the ones we hail

Am
Are the worst of all

F
And the blood's run stale.

Pre-Chorus 1

C
I want to hide the truth,

G
I want to shelter you

Am
But with the beast inside

F
There's nowhere we can hide.

cont.

C
No matter what we breed

G
We still are made of greed.

Am
This is my kingdom come,

F
This is my kingdom come.

Chorus

C
When you feel my heat,

G
Look into my eyes.

Am
It's where my demons hide,

F
It's where my demons hide.

C
Don't get too close,

G
It's dark inside.

Am
It's where my demons hide.

F
It's where my demons hide.

Verse 2

C
When the curtain's call

G
Is the last of all

Am
When the lights fade out

F
All the sinners crawl

C
So they dug your grave

G
And the masquerade

Am
Will come calling out

F
At the mess you made.

Pre-Chorus 2

C
Don't want to let you down

G
But I am hell bound.

Am
Though this is all for you,

F
Don't want to hide the truth.

C
No matter what we breed,

G
We still are made of greed.

Am
This is my kingdom come.

F
This is my kingdom come.

Chorus

C
When you feel my heat,

G
Look into my eyes.

Am
It's where my demons hide,

F
It's where my demons hide.

C
Don't get too close,

G
It's dark inside.

Am
It's where my demons hide,

F
It's where my demons hide.

Bridge

C
They say it's what you make,

G
I say it's up to fate.

Am
It's woven in my soul,

F
I need to let you go.

C
Your eyes, they shine so bright,

G
I want to save their light.

Am
I can't escape this now,

F
Unless you show me how.

Chorus

C
When you feel my heat,

G
Look into my eyes.

Am
It's where my demons hide,

F
It's where my demons hide.

C
Don't get too close,

G
It's dark inside.

Am
It's where my demons hide,

F
It's where my demons hide.

HEY, SOUL SISTER

WORDS AND MUSIC BY PAT MONAHAN, ESPEN LIND AND AMUND BJORKLUND

> **STRUMMING PATTERNS**
> Single down strums
> D DUDUUDU
> DDU UDU
> DDU

C   G   Am   F

To match original recording, place capo on 4th fret

Intro

	C	G	Am	F
	Hey,	hey,		hey.

Verse 1

C
Your lipstick stains

    G   Am
On the front lobe of my left side brains.

F   C
  I knew I wouldn't forget you

            G
And so I went and let you

          Am   F   G
Blow my mind.

     C
Your sweet moonbeam,

  G   Am
The smell of you in every single dream I dream.

F   C
  I knew when we collided,

              G
You're the one I have decided

        Am   F   G
Who's one of my kind.

Chorus

F
Hey, soul sister,

   G   C
Ain't that Mr. Mister

G   F
On the radio, stereo

          G   C   G
The way you move ain't fair, you know.

F
Hey, soul sister,

G   C
I don't want to miss a

G   F   G
Single thing you do,   tonight.

Interlude

C   G   Am   F
                Hey,   hey,   hey.

Verse 2

C
Just in time,

G
    I'm so glad you have

Am
A one track mind like me.

F   C
    You gave my life direction,

                         G
A game show love connection

            Am
We can't deny.

      C
I'm so obsessed,

G   Am
    My heart is bound to beat right out

C   F
My untrimmed chest.

                  C   G
I believe in you, like a virgin you're Madonna

                        Am
And I'm always gonna wanna

                  F   G
Blow your mind.

                    F
Chorus   Hey, soul sister,

                        G   **C**
             Ain't that Mr. Mister

             G   **F**
             On the radio, stereo

                            G   **C**   **G**
             The way you move ain't fair, you know.

                    F
             Hey, soul sister

                G   **C**
             I don't want to miss a

             G   **F**   **G**
             Single thing you do,   tonight.

                    C
Bridge   Way you can cut a rug,

             G
             Watching you's the only drug I need.

                        Am
             You're so gangster, I'm so thug,

                                F
             You're the only one I'm dreaming of, you see.

             C
                 I can be myself now finally,

             G
                 In fact there's nothing I can't be.

             Am   **F**   **G**
                 I want the world to see you be, with me.

Chorus

F
Hey, soul sister,

  G   C
Ain't that Mr. Mister

G   F
On the radio, stereo

       G   C   G
The way you move ain't fair, you know.

F
Hey, soul sister,

G   C
I don't want to miss a

G   F   G
Single thing you do,   tonight.

Outro

F
Hey, soul sister,

  G   C
I don't want to miss a

G   F   G
Single thing you do,   tonight.

C   G   Am   F   G
       Hey,   hey,   hey.

Tonight.

C   G   Am   F   G
       Hey,   hey,   hey.

  C
Tonight.

ME!

WORDS AND MUSIC BY TAYLOR SWIFT, JOEL LITTLE AND BRENDON URIE

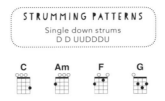

STRUMMING PATTERNS
Single down strums
D D UUDDDU

C   Am   F   G

Intro

N.C.
I promise that you'll never find another like me.

Verse 1

C
I know that I'm a handful, baby, uh.
                                   Am

                               F
I know I never think before I jump

                                    G
And you're the kind of guy the ladies want.

(And there's a lot of cool chicks out there)

C
I know that I went psycho on the phone,
                                  Am

                            F
I never leave well enough alone.

                                 G
And trouble's gonna follow where I go.

(And there's a lot of cool chicks out there)

Pre-Chorus 1

G
But one of these things is not like the others,

Like a rainbow with all of the colors.

Baby doll, when it comes to a lover,

N.C.
I promise that you'll never find another like...

                                C   Am
Chorus 1   Me-e-e, ooh-ooh-ooh-ooh.

                   F
                   I'm the only one of me,

                   G
                   Baby, that's the fun of me.

                                  C   Am
                   Eeh-eeh-eeh, ooh-ooh-ooh-ooh.

                   F
                   You're the only one of you,

                   G
                   Baby, that's the fun of you.

                   N.C.
                   And I promise that nobody's gonna love you like me.

                   C   Am
Verse 2   I know I tend to make it about me,

                                                F
                   I know you never get just what you see

                                        G
                   But I will never bore you, baby.

                   (And there's a lot of lame guys out there)
                   C   Am
                   And when we had that fight out in the rain,

                                                F
                   You ran after me and called my name.

                                        G
                   I never wanna see you walk away.

                   (And there's a lot of lame guys out there)

                   G
Pre-Chorus 2 'Cause one of these things is not like the others,

                   Livin' in winter, I am your summer.

                   Baby doll, when it comes to a lover,
                   N.C.
                   I promise that you'll never find another like...

Chorus 2

            C   **Am**
Me-e-e, ooh-ooh-ooh-ooh.

F
I'm the only one of me,

G
Let me keep you company.

               C   **Am**
Eeh-eeh-eeh, ooh-ooh-ooh-ooh.

F
You're the only one of you,

G
Baby, that's the fun of you.

N.C.
And I promise that nobody's gonna love you like me-e-e.

Bridge

C
Girl, there ain't no 'I' in 'team'

Am
But you know there is a 'me'.

F
Strike the band up, one, two, three.

   G N.C.
I promise that you'll never find another like me.

C
Girl, there ain't no 'I' in 'team'

Am
But you know there is a 'me'.

F
And you can't spell 'awesome' without 'me'.

   G N.C.
I promise that you'll never find another like...

Chorus 3

          C   Am
Me-e-e, (Yeah), ooh-ooh-ooh-ooh (And I want ya, baby).

          F
I'm the only one of me (I'm the only one of me),

          G
Baby, that's the fun of me (Baby, that's the fun of me).

                    C
Eeh-eeh-eeh, ooh-ooh-ooh-ooh (Oh).

          Am
You're the only one of you,

          F
Baby, that's the fun of you.

                 N.C.
And I promise that nobody's gonna love you like me-e-e.

Outro

          C
Girl, there ain't no I in 'team' (Ooh-ooh-ooh-ooh)

          Am
But you know there is a 'me'.

          F
I'm the only one of me (Oh-oh),

          G
Baby, that's the fun of me.

          C
Strike the band up, one, two, three.

              Am
You can't spell 'awesome' without 'me'.

          F
You're the only one of you,

          G
Baby, that's the fun of you.

          N.C.
And I promise that nobody's gonna love you like me-e-e.

I'M YOURS

WORDS AND MUSIC BY JASON MRAZ

> **STRUMMING PATTERNS**
> Single down strums
> UDUX
> DDU UDU

C   G   Am   F   D7

Intro | C | G | Am | F ||

Verse 1

          C
Well, you done, done me in, you bet I felt it,

    G
I tried to be chill but you're so hot that I melted.

   Am   F
I fell right through the cracks, and now I'm trying to get back.

            C
Before the cool done run out, I'll be giving it my bestest,

     G
And nothing's going to stop me but divine intervention,

   Am   F
I reckon it's again my turn to win some or learn some.

Chorus 1

        C   G   Am
But I won't hesitate no more, no more,

              F   C   G
It cannot wait, I'm yours,   mmm.

  Am   F
Hey,   hey.

Verse 2

```
        C                                            G
        Well, open up your mind and see like me,

                                          Am
        Open up your plans and, damn, you're free.

                                          F
        Look into your heart and you'll find love, love, love, love.
        C                                            G
        Listen to the music of the moment people dance and sing;

                          Am
        We're just one big family

        And it's our God-forsaken right to be
        F                        D7
        Loved, loved, loved, loved, loved.
```

Chorus 2

```
        C          G          Am
        So I won't hesitate no more, no more,

                   F
        It cannot wait, I'm sure.
                   C          G          Am
        There's no need to complicate, our time is short,
                   F
        This is our fate, I'm yours.
```

Bridge

```
        C                    G
        Do ya, do, do, do you,   but do ya, do ya, do, do.
        Am                          G              F
        But do you want to come and   scooch on over closer, dear,
                          D7
        And I will nibble your ear.

        Soo, dee, wah, wah, boom, ba,
        C     G
        Bom.  Woah.
        Am    G          F
        Woah, oh, oh, oh, oh, oh.
                  D7
        Uh, huh, mmm.
```

Verse 3   **C**

I've been spending way too long checking my tongue in the mirror,

      G

And bending over backwards just to try to see it clearer

      Am   **F**

But my breath fogged up the glass and so I drew a new face and I laughed.

      C

I guess what I been saying is there ain't no better reason

      G

To rid yourself of vanity and just go with the seasons,

      Am   **F**

It's   what we aim to do, our name is our virtue.

                          C   **G**   **Am**

Chorus 3   But I won't hesitate no more, no more,

                   F

It cannot wait, I'm yours.

            C   **G**

Verse 4   Well, open up your mind and see like me,

                             Am

Open up your plans and, damn, you're free.

                             F

Look into your heart and you'll find that the sky is yours.

      C

So please don't, please don't, please don't.

      G   **Am**

There's no need to complicate 'cause our time is short.

                           F   **D7**

This, oh, this, oh, this is our fate, I'm yours.

Outro   ‖: **C** | **G** | **Am** | **F**   :‖

OCEAN EYES

WORDS AND MUSIC BY FINNEAS O'CONNELL

STRUMMING PATTERNS
Single down strums
DD UU DU UDU UDU
DDU U DU UDU UDU
Pluck strings 3, 1

C   D   Em

Verse 1

I've been watching you

C   D   Em
For some time.

C   D   Em
Can't stop staring

     G   C
At those ocean eyes.

C   D   Em
Burn-ing cities

    C D   Em
And na-palm skies.

C   D   Em   G   C
Fif-teen flares inside those ocean eyes.

  G   C
Your ocean eyes.

Chorus

     C D Em   C D Em
No fair,

            C   D   Em
You really know how to make me cry

                 G   C
When you gimme those ocean eyes.

       C   D   Em   C D Em
I'm scared,

          C   D   Em
I've never fallen from quite this high,

         G   C
Falling into your ocean eyes.

     G   C
Those ocean eyes.

Verse 2

C   D   Em
I've been walking through

    C   D   Em
A world gone blind.

C   D   Em   G   C
Can't stop thinking of your diamond mind.

C   D   Em
Care-ful creature

      C   D   Em
Made friends with time.

     C D Em   G   C
He left her lonely with a diamond mind

         G   C
And those ocean eyes.

Chorus

        C   D   Em   C   D   Em

No fair,

                     C   D   Em

You really know how to make me cry

                              G   C

When you gimme those ocean eyes.

        C   D   Em   C   D   Em

I'm scared,

                  C   D   Em

I've never fallen from quite this high,

                     G   C

Falling into your ocean eyes.

        G   C

Those ocean eyes.

Instrumental   *As Chorus*

Chorus

        C   D   Em   C   D   Em

No fair,

                     C   D   Em

You really know how to make me cry

                              G   C

When you gimme those ocean eyes.

        C   D   Em   C   D   Em

I'm scared,

                  C   D   Em

I've never fallen from quite this high,

                     G   C

Falling into your ocean eyes.

        G   C

Those ocean eyes.

OVER THE RAINBOW

MUSIC BY HAROLD ARLEN
LYRIC BY E.Y. "YIP" HARBURG

> STRUMMING PATTERNS
> Single down strums
> DDU UDU

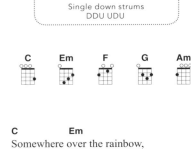

C   Em   F   G   Am

Chorus 1

C   Em
Somewhere over the rainbow,

F   C
Way up high

F   C
And the dreams that you dream of

G   Am
Once in a lullaby.

F
Oh.

Chorus 2

C   Em
Somewhere over the rainbow,

F   C
Bluebirds fly

F   C
And the dreams that you dream of

G   Am
Dreams really do come true.

F
Oh.

Verse 1

         C
Someday, I wish upon a star,

G   Am   F
Wake up where the clouds are far behind   me.

         C
Where trouble melts like lemon drops,

G
High above the chimney top,

     Am   F
That's where you'll find me.

Chorus 3

     C   Em
Somewhere over the rainbow,

F   C
  Bluebirds fly

F   C
And the dreams that you dare to,

G   Am
Oh why, oh why can't I?

F
Oh.

Verse 2

         C
Someday, I wish upon a star,

G   Am   F
Wake up where the clouds are far behind   me.

         C
Where trouble melts like lemon drops,

G
High above the chimney top,

     Am   F
That's where you'll find me

Chorus 4

> C   Em
> Somewhere over the rainbow,
>
> F   C
> Way up high
>
> F   C
> And the dreams that you dare to,
>
> G   Am
> Why, oh why can't I?
>
> F
> I...

Instrumental *As Chorus*

PHOTOGRAPH

WORDS AND MUSIC BY ED SHEERAN, JOHNNY MCDAID,
MARTIN PETER HARRINGTON AND TOM LEONARD

STRUMMING PATTERNS

Single down strums
DDDDDDD
DDU UDU
Chorus: D UUD UU DDU

C   Am   G   F

To match original recording, place capo on 4th fret

Intro | C | | Am | |

| G | | F | |

Verse 1

            C   Am
Loving can hurt, loving can hurt sometimes
            G   F
But it's the only thing that I know.
                    C   Am
When it gets hard, you know it can get hard sometimes.
            G   F
It is the only thing makes us feel alive.

Pre-Chorus 1

        Am   F
We keep this love in a photograph,
    C   G
We made these memories for ourselves.
            Am
Where our eyes are never closing,
    F
Hearts are never broken
            C   G
And time's forever frozen still.

Chorus 1

C
So you can keep me

G
Inside the pocket of your ripped jeans.

Am
Holding me closer 'til our eyes meet,

F
You won't ever be alone, wait for me to come home.

Verse 2

C   Am
Loving can heal, loving can mend your soul

G   F
And it's the only thing that I know, know.

C
I swear it will get easier,

Am
Remember that with ev'ry piece of you.

G   F
Hm, and it's the only thing we take with us when we die.

Pre-Chorus 2

Am   F
We keep this love in a photograph,

C   G
We made these memories for ourselves.

Am
Where our eyes are never closing,

F
Hearts are never broken

C   G
And time's forever frozen still.

Chorus 2

C
So you can keep me

G
Inside the pocket of your ripped jeans.

Am
Holding me closer 'til our eyes meet,

F
You won't ever be alone, wait for me to come home.

34

                                   C

Chorus/Outro And if you hurt me,

                                               G

That's okay, baby, only words bleed.

                                       Am

Inside these pages you just hold me

                               F

And I won't ever let you go.

                           Am

Wait for me to come home.

                           F

Wait for me to come home.

                           C

Wait for me to come home.

                           G

Wait for me to come home.

                        C

Oh, you can fit me

                                                     G

Inside the necklace you got when you were sixteen.

                                         Am

Next to your heartbeat where I should be,

                               F

Keep it deep within your soul.

                         C

And if you hurt me,

                                       G

Well, that's okay, baby, only words bleed.

                                       Am

Inside these pages you just hold me

                               F

And I won't ever let you go.

                         C   **G**

When I'm away, I will remember how you kissed me

                               Am

Under the lamppost back on Sixth street.

                                       F

Hearing you whisper through the phone,

                               C

'Wait for me to come home'.

SHAPE OF YOU

WORDS AND MUSIC BY ED SHEERAN, KEVIN BRIGGS,
KANDI BURRUSS, TAMEKA COTTLE, STEVE MAC AND JOHNNY MCDAID

STRUMMING PATTERNS
Single down strums
D UDU DU
DD U UDU
Pluck string 4 UX

Am   Dm   F   G

To match original recording, place capo on 4th fret

Intro | Am | Dm | F | G ||

Verse 1

      Am   Dm
The club isn't the best place to find a lover,

      F   G
So the bar is where I go.

Am   Dm
Me and my friends at the table doing shots,

      F   G
Drinking fast and then we talk slow.

      Am   Dm
And you come over and start up a conversation with just me,

      F   G
And trust me I'll give it a chance, now.

      Am   Dm
Take my hand, stop, put Van The Man on the jukebox,

      F   G
And then we start to dance and now I'm singing like:

Pre-chorus 1

                      Am   Dm
            'Girl, you know I want your love,

            F   G   Am
            Your love was handmade for somebody like me.

                        Dm
            Come on now, follow my lead,

            F   G
            I may be crazy, don't mind me.

                 Am   Dm
            Say, boy, let's not talk too much,

            F   G   Am
            Grab on my waist and put that body on me.

                        Dm
            Come on now, follow my lead,

                    F   G
            Come, come on now, follow my lead.'

Chorus 1

              Am   Dm   F
                  I'm in love with the shape of you,

                        G   Am
            We push and pull like a magnet do.

                      Dm   F
            Although my heart is falling too,

                  G   Am
            I'm in love with your body.

                    Dm   F
                Last night you were in my room,

                    G   Am
            And now my bedsheets smell like you.

                        Dm   F
            Every day discovering something brand new,

                    G
            Oh, I'm in love with your body.

Chorus 2

Am   Dm
Oh, I, oh, I, oh, I, oh, I,

F   G
    Oh, I'm in love with your body.

Am   Dm
Oh, I, oh, I, oh, I, oh, I,

F   G
    Oh, I'm in love with your body.

Am   Dm
Oh, I, oh, I, oh, I, oh, I,

F   G
    Oh, I'm in love with your body.

Am   Dm   F
    Every day discovering something brand new,

        G
I'm in love with the shape of you.

Verse 2

Am   Dm
One week in we let the story begin,

            F   G
We're going out on our first date.

        Am   Dm
You and me are thrifty, so go all you can eat,

            F   G
Fill up your bag and I fill up a plate.

           Am   Dm
We talk for hours and hours about the sweet and the sour,

            F   G
And how your family is doing okay.

           Am   Dm
And leave and get in a taxi, then kiss in the backseat,

         F   G
Tell the driver make the radio play, and I'm singing like:

Pre-chorus 2   *as Pre-chorus 1*

Chorus 3   *as Chorus 1*

Chorus 4   *as Chorus 2*

N.C.

Bridge   Come on, be my baby, come on.

Come on, be my baby, come on.

Come on, be my baby, come on.

Come on, be my baby, come on.

Am   **Dm**
Come on, be my baby, come on.

F   **G**
Come on, be my baby, come on.

Am   **Dm**
Come on, be my baby, come on.

N.C.
Come on, be my baby, come on.

Chorus 5   *as Chorus 1*

Am   **Dm**
Chorus 6   (Come on, be my baby, come on.)

F   **G**
(Come on) I'm in love with your body.

Am   **Dm**
(Come on, be my baby, come on.)

F   **G**
(Come on) I'm in love with your body.

Am   **Dm**
(Come on, be my baby, come on.)

F   **G**
(Come on) I'm in love with your body.

Am   **Dm**   **F**
Every day discovering something brand new,

            G
I'm in love with the shape of you.

ALSO AVAILABLE ONLINE AND FROM ALL GOOD MUSIC SHOPS...

ORDER No. AM1012000

ORDER No. AM1013232

ORDER No. HLE90004959

ORDER No. AM1013067

ORDER No. HL00287157

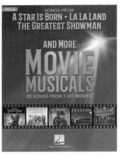

ORDER No. HL00287578

ORDER No. HL00290992

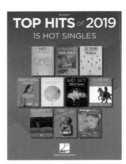

ORDER No. HL00301152

ORDER No. HL00149250

Just visit your local music shop and ask
to see our huge range of music in print.